Not A Monolith

Not A Monolith

Not A Monolith:

poems and musings of a black woman

By

Shantasha Naomi Laing

Not A Monolith:

poems and musings of a black woman

Second Edition

Book Cover by Chelsea Simone

Dedicated to the multifaceted.

Acknowledgments

For Zina; forever loving, the most resilient person I know. Epitome of an empath
Imoni; for your continued support and often harassment. I respect and adore you.
Dashari; my chosen brother and confidante. Let's continue to dive deep.
Nelson; my literal day 1 supporter. Thank you for always believing in my craft.
Chels; a true artist and overall good human, you continue to inspire me.
& Roger; for just letting me be. You've been my rock.
&& Luci; the coolest girl I know, I love you.

Thank you.

Table of Contents

Dear Reader,

Table of Contents

Thank you, and Welcome to *Not A Monolith*. This project
revealed itself sometime in early 2020 —both in the quiet
and the madness of that year. As the death toll steadily
climbed in the forefront of lives while the battle for
black lives was being broadcasted for all to see, I became
enraged at the world around me. I returned to what I've
always known: writing. Whether it be diary entries,
essays, stories, and eventually poems…, the written word
has always allowed me to center myself.

Over the next three years, I would struggle with
depression, anxiety, and general dissatisfaction with the
state of the world like millions of others. I took many
hiatuses while creating this project and thought this idea
might never materialize. But I knew I had to publish this
works, as it firmly planted itself in my psyche; not a day
could pass without me thinking about *Not A Monolith*. The
intention behind *Not A Monolith* is to express an authentic
range of life experiences through the cultural lens of a
black woman. Throughout these four sections, my hope is
that you discover relatable stories. I dream that *Not A
Monolith: poems and musings of a black woman* contributes
to the greater phenomenon we find ourselves in again- A
Black Renaissance.

With Love,

Shantasha Naomi Laing

(Love & love adjacent)

The Sun is on my payroll

There is no other explanation for the way I
radiate so brilliantly under his gaze.
Gilded threads weave between sheets of
toasted melanin.

And I, wholly displayed.

Completely devoted to his earthly goddess

Enjoying his warmth from our first embrace

captivated

Hopeful that in return- he may bask in my
glory.

In hopes that I'll acknowledge his
magnificent works.

Need to feel the romance of my pen
The lamp's soft orange glow
Lotioned skin
Comforting wafts of sandalwood
Invites me to move
Gliding in
And up
And out
And down
Until completion

A poet's night in

The leaves were yellow

The leaves were yellow
The sky was blue
Skin honeyed
The air clear
An exhale when kisses draw near.
Full brown warm kisses
Accompanied by new adventures
And long loving stares.
Blow heat upon mahogany-hued cheeks

I used to pray for the day my dreams would end.
      An image of you lain between my thighs
           still tortuously lingers
                    behind.

Afterimage

But to be in love is lovely,
No matter how hard I try to
convince myself otherwise.

-musings #17/hardtruths

Heart Scars

A corner of my heart beats
for you,
And
Through these valves- I'll
bleed for you

we're in mourning, she and I

Forged with falling embers
Yours imprints on mine

Here lies our hopelessness,
Our triumphs…

A rawness,
I fear will never return.

I keep forgetting we're not in
love anymore.

-musings #14/love-nesia

naiveté

I loved you,
When I had no business doing so.
I was but a husk,
Pouring out of nothingness.
Ohhh, but did I love you fiercely!
I gave you part of my essence.
And I grew weary,
As I steadily poured…

You never asked for it
but needed love anyway.
Awakening a martyr in me—
who loved unconditionally.

Even if that meant self-sacrifice.

If I had all the time in the world, I would
spend it with my friends.

-musings #23/ soulmates

Life in the in-betweens

The soft whirl from a ceiling fan
at the end of the day.
Embrace the comfort of an oversized cotton tee.

after the heat of a warm shower.

Take a beat, smile in the mirror
Bathe in your own ambiance.
Admire the idiosyncrasies of your face,
Soak it all in.

Laugh until you cry
Bear witness to life
Here and now
Be present in all your transitions.

Experience life...*always*

Anchored, feeling safe with you.
Afloat choppy waters, I'd rather stay with you.

-musings #19/into the calm

Drawn to you like a moth to a flame.
Captured by your deceptive glow.
Pulled away from my path.
better off sifting through the darkness alone.

lustful lenses

I want you… even when our body heat swells, pull me in closer.

-musings #22/night sweats

The push and pull fills me with unburdened bliss.
Fervent tingle of an unknown known.
Like a perfectly timed meal,
In an otherwise unpredictable day.
Delectably familiar
Unsurprisingly intimate.
Flesh demands more flesh,
But all good meals must come to an end.

First time in forever

Love should be fun.
Bring forward our true selves.
Nurture them and in return- they'll inspire you.
Find joy in the mundane
And glee in the heavy.

Love is imaginative.
Play make-believe; dress
up.
Share wild dreams, giggle about silly crushes.
Time travel to your mother's kitchen through nostalgic
flavors.

To love is to be human.
I am Love.

Love is

Safe Haven

Let me lay on your chest.
never felt this safe around a man before.
You're strong without trying—
My safe house.

But I crave you in other ways
Your lips on those lips
Your face brushed against these thighs

A lift in my chest,
exhale
my breathy cadence quickens.

With every tender kiss
From your pillowy lips,
My body releases unto you.

Ambrosia to the gods

Highly sought after.
Feed only the worthy.

The leaves are yellow, part 2

Anger, you and I cannot coexist!
Like leaves falling in autumn
I admire our death

We released each other like changing seasons
Slowly at first, then suddenly the air chilled
Our leaves settled
And the love between us becomes the nutrients
For two new lovers next spring

I think I'd love you in any form.
-musings #24/ even in friendship

The Sun Has A Romantic Side

Kisses in the sun
Rays of sunshine lightly warm my cheek.
Eyelids maroon and softly closed.
As lips instinctively part.
Graciously thanking the sun
for setting the mood.

Worship me!

I'm not saying it's right.
but damn does it feel good.

-musings #2/ kink beginnings

gifted.

Love the black man.
Caress his head as he drops asleep
between thick thighs- color of cognac.
Same thighs- stubborn as tree trunks
and dense as memory foam.

love the black man.
Pour forth intuition
like sun-warmed cocoa butter,
Left ajar in a blindless room.

love the black man.
Embrace him in laughter
because with *you*
Moments feel joyous.

love the black man.
foster his vulnerability,
black liberation lies just
beyond the veil.

I *want* to love the black man… I really do.

The Blues

I thought i should write this before the meds kick in.
panicked that i'll never find that *oomph* again.
nothing I write seems extraordinary; everything feels
contrived...
My mental illness is not my talent.
My anxiety doesn't strengthen my craft.
My depression isn't artsy,
and yet…

…Pending

You declare protection.

Yet it is us who are left cowering in the streets.
Left to live with the PTSD of all the women before
and all…

the women who will tragically befriend the wrong man,
walk down a wrong path, drink the wrong drink, wear
the wrong dress, say the wrong thing… and will it be
you that makes it right?

Will it be you who holds friends
accountable? Or is it all pageantry?

Make a safe space for u

*lease. I would like- no, I need you to shut the fuck up.

-musings #8/OVersTimuLAteD

journey beyond self

I didn't know my trauma
Totally unaware of the damage inflicted,
Blissfully ignorant to my situation.

The mind, terrifying and powerful.
It has the power to destroy
And power to uplift
The power to enslave
And power to set free
Cunning enough to confuse
Clever enough to succeed

Restrained by fears
I've yet to set myself free
Still on a journey to find what lies
beyond the trauma.

Am I depressed or is it these birth control side effects?

-musings #16/ this or that

There are not enough words
from my history,
Or gallons of water
Not enough salt in the sea,
Or white candles
Not enough incense,
Or moments of silence
Not enough rationale,
Or genuine support

That'll release me from this loss.

This pain will live in the walls of my body
Restructured into my cells.
I've made my commitment to healing
For I will never be *healed* from
this.

ripped apart.

loss

Not sure if the antidepressants worked today?
-musings #15/finally medicated

Death & rebirth of a friendship

Your weekly, and often daily presence is missed.
days are filled with too much reason.
You were kinetic energy.

Being around you was a jolt to try
anything.
To be everything.

You probably thought I didn't care,
But what's the use reaching out-
To be hurt again?
You always pulled my raw emotions

You saw a glimpse of my shadows
And I saw yours,

I don't know what we had
but I know it is not over
Our friendship will keep changing like the seasons
Always changing yet ever consistent.

Living shouldn't be so hard, so why the hell is it?

-musings #6/ (internal scream)

Bring me the happy

If only I could find a way
to extend these days of happiness.
Curiously wondering,
Do happy people exist?

When I find myself in a time—
Times when my heart isn't heavy.
When my body ain't *so* tense.
A moment when anxiety decides, it too needs a
breather.
Bles-sed peace washes over me.

How hopeful that'll find happiness *over* and
over and *over* again.
How Very Hopeful

If I must apologize to another white man...
In the most dramatic way possible... *IT IS KILLING ME*.

-musing #1/side effects might include death

Every day I mumble to myself, "are you unwell?" in
response to a rabid adult customer.

-musings #9/ adult temper tantrums

exhausted

So god damn tired.

Too tired to even write this-
This fucking poem.

For surely, it has some better-suited name.
But I'm too damn tired to think about it.

A weariness settles into my bones
Like an over-steeped tea bag.
Because even brewed tea becomes another task,
In a long list of many many tasks,
On an ever-growing list of shit to do.

Like coals in a slow-roasting flame
And I, the pig, being burned evenly from every side.

Packed bags and broken promises

Packed bags and broken promises create hard little
girls.

My dad couldn't honor them- creating sad little
girls.

That said, jokes in fatherin' 'came our little
world.

My dad sick of arguing with five little girls.

Not *all* bad, gifts and promises gave hope to his
girls.
A fun dad, unfit for fathering strong daughters
in his world.

Still loved dad through broken promises, creating
disappointed little girls.

You keep swallowing the pain!
No wonder it hurts to speak.
          -musings #28/ wringing my own neck

Fear is setting in.
I know what I have to do.
Still frightened, at that.

Haiku for Fear

If I were a white woman

If I were a white woman,
I'd float by on mediocracy.
I'd take subpar humor
And rise the ranks of comedienne.
Or maybe my *girl next door* looks
would land me high-paid commercial gigs.
Better yet, maybe I'd become a model, uniqueness replaced by
palatable whiteness, european ancestry, and a symmetrical
enough face.

If I were a white woman,
I'd have not grown up questioning my desirability…
By boys my shade and darker.
Deep down I would know I am *the standard*, the norm
affirmed by society's gaze.

If I were a white woman,
And things weren't going my way…
I would simply cry.
Big, flagrant, theatrical gold.
Comforted by the fact…somebody would answer for their crimes
against me.
Consoled by the fact that I would never truly answer for
mine.

If I were a white woman,
I could be emotionally dishonest.
As I march for a cause,
Then return home to kiss the lips of the exact type of man
responsible for the very injustice I supposedly detest.
I would have found conviction in a difference of opinion.

If I were a white woman
I would have successfully deluded myself.
Preaching feminism while actively pillaging black women…
time and time again.
Never feeling shame unless exposed.
Never feeling remorse unless affected.

But I'm a black woman, so let me get my ass to work

Patriarchy spreads its miasma through the very fabric of our lives.

    -musings #20/ poisonous

...now you don't

Measured by meaningless metrics.
Capitalism, our contemporary captor, chips away at me
steadily.
Patiently planning my escape

Prefer my pain behind closed doors
My entire life is not up for
exhibition.

-musings #18/ semi-open book

Maybe if I were a dog... just maybe...
-musings #3/even the dogs have rights

The Breaking Point

be free.

The alternative is lethal.
There is so much more.
Culture, philosophy
curiosity is waiting on *us*.
How much longer can we endure this continued
imprisonment?

among the tortured
Who realized... *this* is not living.

we've been drowning for so long-been trapped for so long

Hear them whispering "please rest."

Community

Black excellence wanes, there is celebration in
just...*being*

-musings #26/simply existing

Instant Familiarity

Enter to sounds of an old bashment mix
Envelopes lay across the passenger seat
Lotto tickets jut outta the sun visor
A little black tree swings off the faded rearview
mirror

Our first encounter
community already shared.
Not a word uttered.
Thank you for safe passage, unc.

I cried as the ground kissed my feet. Blades of grass
licked at my soles.
Memories, the refreshing kind
Stood at attention.

Cousins licking popsicles over they favorite auntie
house- the one with the good snacks,
On an otherwise unbearably hot day. days like this
where the sun beats on you. Like your cousin that
plays too damn much.

I rip the blades of grass in between my toes
Memories interwoven between my muscles,
band together
Now.
Serenity finds me in folded blades of grass pressed
against the pads of my feet.

Using the earth for a gentle release.
My feet have seen it all.
Stomping for mercifulness
I have not yet shown myself mercy.

Tethered

A great writer once said, "a nigger in business is a terrible thing", I think about this often…

-musings #13/ Ms. Toni Knew

No permission

slips needed

Let black women be

    Weird
    & loud
    & smart
    & ghetto
    & shy
    & dumb
    & soft
    & sassy
    & depressed
    & successful
    & thriving
    & simple
    & talented
    & extra
    & quiet
    & unfriendly
    & affectionate
    & funny

    & Every fucking thing else

They shall appear

Sometimes we forget the power of our own tongue.
How many times have we spoken life into the unknown?
Forge certainty from the uncertain.
Our tongue, a tool of unimaginable influence

A weapon to yield brilliantly.

Getting complimented at the gas
station.

-musings #21/ a black girl's universal experience

Blackity Black

Make mine extra black
Nothings too much when it comes down to us.
Long curved nails with rhinestones and chains,
applaud the ceremonial click-clack of a full set.
Neon-colored hair on dark-skinned girls with
effervescent white smiles.
so pretty in pink
The best the color ever did wear.

 A gold-toothed auntie dressed in a mischievous smile
 with a
heart of...polished gold
 And a sickening 27-piece to match.
 Adorned with an ass -only a cookout veteran achieves.

Mathematically guided straight backs.
Curriculum-worthy parts,
strands of hair spun into ropes of silk.

Pressed-down durags and puffed-up bonnets.
Waves with no water
Juice with no cups
Adorned in jewelry from tip to toe

Unbridled in blackness.

Cup is full

My life is full of cheer.
Full of newborn smell and little wisps of hair.

Full of laughter
Full of friends
Full of family shenanigans

Full of feeling
Joy and grief
Fullness fills my grounded feet.

Full of silly
Full of woe

and never fully in the know.

An open book test y'all still managed to fail.
-musings #7/thoughts on blackfishing

Represent

To see it is to dream it
That's all it takes.
Fostered dreams turn into reality.
Untapped potential is our communal mistake.

"Representation matters" not a flippant phrase
Kids need it reflected to their face.

The child that never sees a blown balloon…
How do they become a balloon artist?

He gingerly placed his hands on her cheek.
Aware that his fingers were not combs to
rake through such full & kinky hair.

 -musings #12/A Black YA Encounter

A *sinner's prayer*

It starts with a compulsory act.
How natural the feeling

How easily I recall, it's muscle memory now.
With closed eyes and a bowed head

alongside family gathered around a table
A memory bordering a distant daydream.

Shouts of excitement from kids buzzing with energy
Over dishes prepared with care.
taste the love in this meal tonight.

Oh what a lovely vision…
It fades as I acknowledge the dead silence only living
alone
can provide.
Appreciating *this* meal made for me, by me.

inviting grace; accepting the here and now.
This must be honored by prayer.

Amen.

                              Unquestionable.

                  no denying my blackness.
                      no cold winters or
                  hot summers spent indoors
                  could alter my appearance.
         My blackness on center stage- eternally.
          The audience and its captive performer
Whether I was up for the performance or not.

They will never let you be white, and you
won't accept you're forever gonna be black…
-musings #25/concerned about coons

traffic jam

I know a girl so fine, see her out here causin' traffic
Every unc n' phew
Breakin' necks just to get a view

ain't smiling, eyes straight, her head on a swivel
Eyes grew in the back of her head before her first
barbaric whistle

boys turned disobedient dogs
Barking at her - ain't no home training,
Them boys was parented all wrong.

Gotta watch out for the strays
dogs are just as thirsty in the wintertime
Watch out he'll be begging for days
He doesn't see harassment as a crime.

I don't love america, but I love New Orleans
people are so warm- voices make strangers feel like family
Food that nourishes - spirits that energize till I'm
greeted by dawn.

Don't care for america, but Brooklyn is a shining star.
The passion- an effortless cool… parties that
feel cinematic with DJs who know what to play!

Don't fuck with Texas, but Houston got it going on.
Big, brown and bold
Where women are healthy - looking fine as ever.

Don't support florida, but Orlando is home.
Caribbeans are near, Latinos plentiful,
Asians stay chefin.
Food authentic from kitchens where care stays present.

I love (my) America

Oh, can't talk right now. Acrylics got me feeling godly.

-musings #4/fresh set

I love all my bitches

I love my bitches petite,
I love my bitches thick,
longways and sideways
big booties and small tits.

I love my bitches Amazonian,
Like fucking majestic giraffes.
I love my bitches flat or plump,
Both back and from the front.

I love my bitches dark
with iridescent hues.
Like amethyst and obsidian crystals
Swirled and cleaved into two.

I love my bitches light
Like golden little nugs.
I love my bitches brown like me
Face the sun from above.

I love all my bitches.
And all my bitches love me.
Honored to be a part of gang,
The prettiest family.

Speak to me softly

We are allowed our full range of emotions.
Were we not born into this world squishy and
delicate?
And screaming?
This perceived strength
does not negate my actual *softness*.
A myriad of emotions
Flow through all of us.
And as I lean into femininity
Ready yourself to receive me
Don't forget when you part your lips
Speak to me softly.

After ancient Africa shit got really really

weird.

-musings #11/we have the tools

It is that simple act of protection
The last defense of the day.
Grease that scalp, get some rest.

-musings #5/ bonnet & durag love

now I know my affirmations

Amazing as she is.
Beautiful as she is.
Creative as she is.
Damning as she is.
Ethereal as she is.
Forgiving as she is.
Generous as she is.
Hilarious as she is.
Intelligent as she is.
Joyful as she is.
Knowledgeable as she is.
Lovely as she is.
Maleficent as she is.
Notorious as she is.
Omnipotent as she is.
Peculiar as she is.
Quick-witted as she is.
Radiant as she is.
Stylish as she is.
Tenacious as she is.
Underrated as she is.
Victorious as she is.
Xenial as she is.
Youthful as she is.
Zany as she is.

        Keep going.

Siren's epic

Ooh how good it feels to be me!
Pussy fresh
purred, and pretty.

Panties picked with audience anticipation.

Ass perched like a peach.
Pressed against a little black dress.
Each stride alarming, panic upon every
step.

Heavy-lined lips
plumped and puckered.
Eyebrows plucked and arched.

Eyeliner attentively applied.

She parts the crowd in any space.
Admirers gawk, pulled in by her aroma.
Bewitched by her allure.

plotting or praising as she breezes by…

Roots

Summers in Florida

Sunrays shine through slits of outdated
curtains. Granny's mango tree sways out the
corner of my eye.
An audible hum from an overworked a/c unit
buzzes in the background.

The heat presses through my windowpane.
Charming.

In its own way…

June is for Fam(ily)

Palm trees wave *hello*
Gran's mangoes are sweet.
With sticky hands we laugh
Joking with each other, the only way families
can.
Through multi-layered inside jokes
Intergenerational friendship treasured.
At our best, stuffed full in front of a meal.
Everything is sweeter in the summer.
Family gatherings, forever spirited
Softened by muggy, summery late nights

Let us feast on the vibrancy of life!
Enjoying this familial season.
Let our soundtrack be laughter and disagreements.
Our bodies are filled with abundant energy

And unwound by bountiful rest.

Ears perk up when I hear that bass boomin from down
the street.

-musings #27/ quite literally turn that shit up!

Twenty -six

Felt a lot older than I imagined
How can life be so hard?
For someone still so young
Maybe cause I've been aging for so long.
aches echo the trauma stored in my bones.

My 26
Feels the pressure of parenting for my
siblings
When my mother was…
Erranding
Socializing
Selling
Working
Partying
Fighting
Arguing
Selling
Partying
Yelling
Crying
Selling

My 26
Feels the strain in my throat
As I stand up to my father for the first
time

My 26

Feels the shame of a 16-year-old
hyperventilating behind closed doors too
embarrassed for familial eyes.

My 26
Remembers too many moments of chaos.

Two young dumb parents, morphing my

molding mind.

My 26

Well, my 26 is tired.

Croissants in the Park

Memories begrudgingly start to fade.
But croissants in the park are as
vibrant as ever.
Faint smells from the bakery
as we stroll side by side.
Today we make sandwiches on croissants.

Today's not cold
no not at all.
The sun lightly sweeps through the streets.
I think we could still wear a thin
cardigan, perhaps.
Memory becomes unreliable with finer details such as this.

But I do remember seeing lots of green.
Surrounded by lots of rays.
Looking up into the most graceful face.
This memory, no matter how faded
Will live on forever.

Sun outside my granny's house shines
brighter, grass is always greener.

-musings #23/granny's home

Growing up other

There were very few moments that I felt
Ugly.
I thank the matriarchs of my life for their lent
confidence.
Despite this critical head start, my battle against
insidious beauty standards would rage on.

That feeling of *other* successfully masks itself,
Especially to this young black girl.

Who walked into classrooms plunged in a
Sea of blondes and brunettes,
Straight, "curly" and wavy - biologically *relaxed.*
Fair, olive, tan, and profoundly different than me.
My otherness exemplified in every peer I see.

As if my skin was darker under those school
fluorescents.
As if my permed hair
shrieked imposter as new growth drew a line in the sand
between me and *them.*
As if my home customs were in any way
shameful.

Over and over, rinse and repeat.
Even my mother's reassurance felt no louder than a
whisper in the cacophony of youth.

So, celebration must be boisterous!
Self-praise must be unapologetic!
Honoring the little girl who stood alone as

Other.

And we would discover that we'd be sisters in
every timeline and in any world.

-musings #30/ kismet

schools out

Chlorine stripped hair of little mermaids in the
making.
Manic squeals and mad laughter behind every
summer day.

Faded bikini lines that last long after fall.
Slap-slap of flip flops, drag-drag of slides,
Squeak-squeak of fresh sneaks.
The wondrous chorus of youth chants on.

Sandy bums, cheeky attitudes- when moms not close
by.
Hot dogs, hamburgers, ice cream, and a cake
created the summer eats.

A school friend reunion on an unexpected
day. begging for a meet-up outside those school
walls.
Expected afternoon showers, timed so precisely
rarely ever missing a pool day.

Where children swim through humidity and laugh
through sweltering heat.

Dreadful?

They ask me if I'm dreadful?
And I say…
"of course, I am!"

The root behind my dreads
Are dreadful certainly.
A toss of these matted tresses denounces false
beauty standards.
Firmly tells professionalism to fuck off.

My dreads honor the history of men and women before
me.

Reminding me that I am always on a journey.
A sage timekeeper in the making.

Never knew how painfully I craved to be soft.
My mother wanted to protect me- meant well.
But concrete poured where roses would
Bloom
Tears flowed only in secret- publicly choking on
words.

Digging cement is no easy task. Took a few cracks
to break free, now watch me grow.

Tough skin

Breakfast at Grans

"Get up, breakfast is ready"
The day starts abruptly but it's already filled
with love.
breakfast calls are my favorite
"Oh good, grans in a cheerful mood"
This too is a cherished feeling

aroma of ackee & saltfish (ackee picked fresh
from the backyard), steamed callaloo (with just
enough scotch bonnet so my two baby sisters still
enjoy), fried dumpling (I prefer boiled), boiled
banana (a necessary addition), boiled dumpling
(mingling with the banana), fried plantain
(perfectly sweet), festival (a crowd favorite-
deservedly so), and a bit a well-seasoned kidney
(a shared favorite between mommy and me).

mint leaves picked from last Sunday
her herb garden in full bloom.
while we were sleeping the day away
tea brewed and cooled.
the kettle is still warm.
look at this bounty set before us.

Breakfast at Grams

"Get up, breakfast is ready"
The day starts abruptly but it's already filled
with love.
breakfast calls are my favorite
"Oh good, grans in a cheerful mood"
This too is a cherished feeling

aroma of ackee & saltfish (ackee picked fresh
from the backyard), steamed callaloo (with just
enough scotch bonnet so my two baby sisters still
enjoy), fried dumpling (I prefer boiled), boiled
banana (a necessary addition), boiled dumpling
(mingling with the banana), fried plantain
(perfectly sweet) festival (a crowd favorite
deservedly so), and a bit a well-seasoned kidney
(a shared favorite between mommy and me).

mint leaves picked from last Sunday
her herb garden in full bloom.
while we were sleeping the day away
tea brewed and cooled.
the kettle is still warm.
look at this bounty set before us

Shantasha Laing was born in Brampton, Canada,
but primarily raised in Orlando, FL. Oldest of 6
children, Shantasha grew up in a Jamaican
household surrounded by many matriarchs in her
youth. She moved several times during childhood,
attending 16 schools K-8th. Shantasha takes
pride in being a daughter, granddaughter, niece,
friend, confidante, and above all, the eldest
sister and bonus mom to all the wonderful ladies
(and a few special men) in her life. Shantasha
graduated from the University of Florida, where
she obtained a Bachelor's Degree in Health
Science, although her diploma currently collects
dust at her home in Tampa.

Shantasha Laing was born in Brampton, Canada, but primarily raised in Orlando, FL. Oldest of 6 children, Shantasha grew up in a Jamaican household surrounded by many matriarchs in her youth. She moved several times during childhood, attending 16 schools K-8th. Shantasha takes pride in being a daughter, granddaughter, niece, friend, confidante, and above all, the eldest sister and bonus mom to all the wonderful ladies (and a few special men) in her life. Shantasha graduated from the University of Florida, where she obtained a Bachelor's degree in Health Science, although her diploma currently collects dust at her home in Tampa.

48684489R00059